The Elohssa
A Phenomenal Pest

Jorge Rodriguez-Walling

Storybook Cottage—Miami, FL
ISBN: 978-0-692-14773-3
Library of Congress Control Number: (pending)
The Elohssa: A Phenomenal Pest |
Jorge Rodriguez-Walling
Available Formats: eBook | Paperback distribution

A SPECIAL THANKS...

MUST GO OUT TO ALL THE ASSHOLES IN MY
LIFE,
BECAUSE WITHOUT YOUR INSPIRATION
AND LIFETIME EXAMPLES,
THIS BOOK WOULD NOT HAVE BEEN
POSSIBLE.

THANK YOU.

FORWARD

This book and the characters in it are all fictional accounts of a particular kind of person who has always been a perpetual presence in all civilizations. There are no specific names mentioned or photographic visuals provided in this work in order to protect the rights of privacy and the innocent. It is, however, a descriptive account of a generic specie of person who has long survived by his unique talent to annoy others for a lifetime. The subject is treated colloquially, subjectively, even sociologically, in an effort to point out the flawed personality of such a person.

You will also notice that women and children are excluded from the narrative for no other reason than to expose only one kind of prototype personality expressed in the form of a guy and to use this model as examples of his personality traits in society as well as in tighter social circles.

This undertaking is also based on the culmination of my association with many such people throughout my career, interweaving themselves into my life in ways I never anticipated or ever thought possible. I use my personal experiences as an inspiration to create this fictional character with which we all can relate in one way or another. Looking back, the prototype person in question has manipulated my years of professional work quite profoundly, both in the workplace and in the family. And in the middle of it all, I never came to know how to deal with such a person. I didn't have a reference of any kind, never found anyone to talk to about it, and I didn't know how to overcome and supersede such an influence on family, colleagues, personal friends and myself.

This is also the type of book that people won't normally talk about in public or at fancy soirees, but they will certainly love reading and relishing it in private. The public relates to it because it's something relevant in their lives; it's the here and now for them, which also brings them to a "What are we going to do about it" kind of attitude. In short, the courage involved with writing this kind of book goes to the truthful and realistic testament of the leitmotif in our lives, ripping our days moment by moment and leaving us for what's worse than dead: a curator for the *Elohssa*.

It is, therefore, my intention to first make you laugh a bit here and there or at least crack a smile or two along the way, but mostly, it is also intended to make you think about people, about your sense of judgment in selecting your friends, and about the many ways to consider human nature. This book can be a bit strong from time to time, but it's important to make a burly commentary about it based on the many sardonic experiences of my past. So sit back, have some wine, take a drink, or sip on some good coffee and enjoy the book for what it offers: light humor with a twist, yet a tinge of thought.

As a final consideration on your part, if after reading this you should find it to be something relevant in your life, please pass the message onto others who also need to hear and be made aware of such people before they get a chance to do irreparable damage. If you don't find this work useful, put it aside – but I hope you won't. Thanks!

Introduction: A Freak of Nature

Unit 1: Discovering *The Elohssa*

Unit 2: Interacting With *The Elohssa*

Unit 3: Protecting Yourself From *The Elohssa*

INTRODUCTION

A Freak Of Nature

The book you are about to read is unlike any other you've read before. It could be an entertaining read for many, but I treat it as a serious academic issue, a sociological phenomenon that departs from all that is considered convention, and, one which plagues our society when coming into contact with the human interaction of personalities.

We live in a free society, but we also like to think of it as a democracy, and upon further reflection, I guess it is free to the extent that we can each go to different places throughout the day, untethered and without fear of any kind of persecution. We go to work, we go shopping, we travel, we relocate, we go out to dinner, we have our own businesses, we buy and sell properties, and we invest. In short, we can do more things with our living standards than most people are able to do in many other countries. We all go about our lives as if nothing or nobody can interfere with it, but someone does, and always has for a long time now. And though you may not fully recognize him for what he really is, yet, you've always felt this feeling of clutter and confinement by a certain presence never before pinpointed or identified clearly. Well, the feeling is real, not imagined!

And as we continue to enjoy our society freely, we also coexist and mutually tolerate a plethora of other people who have long demanded that our free society be an inclusive one. Inclusiveness invites all kinds of people, as expressed in various races, ethnicities, genders, classes, gays, straights, the maladjusted, the liberals and conservatives, convicted criminals, teenagers, nerds, the arrogant, the coy, the passive-aggressive, the nonconformist, and of course, lets not forget the misfits and loners too. But then, standing alone, separate and apart from everyone else, is the *Elohssa*, a distinct breed of people, to be sure, who also collaborates with the rest of us everyday. A freak product, borne out of the most un-natural order of things in the universe, this contemptible anomaly of humanity is the focus of our study. This book will prove to be ageless because you will always have *Elohssas* afflicting your life. Ok, it's time to meet *The Elohssa*. What is it?

Chapter-1

<u>What Is It?</u>

The *Elohssa,* is an asshole spelled backward as a wayward euphemism for a very disturbed human being, and we are all inundated with them, neck deep! Look, before you go jumping to conclusions about what I'm doing, let me first clarify further the motivation for this work. My use of the word "asshole" in describing a certain prototype of person is not intended to be derogatory or vulgar by way of anyone's interpretation. I chose to use this word because there can be no better word that can best create the image in your mind of a person so distinctly flawed and inadequate that he can easily be considered beyond any and all hope of repair. And while I am well aware of the conversational stereotype it carries, yet, I try to treat the application of the word objectively, almost scientifically, in the way this prototype personality affects our lives.

Perhaps we should start by offering a

definition or some sense of conceptualization about what the asshole is by Geoffrey Nunberg, a University of California at Berkeley linguistic professor and author of *Ascent of the A-Word: Assholism, the First Sixty Years*. He proceeds to describe this person as:

> *"It's somebody who is deliberately obtuse about his rights and entitlements and his relations with other people, who imagines that his position in a marriage, in an office, or on a line, gives him privileges that it doesn't, and someone who ought to know better."*

Nunberg's point is well taken, since the asshole is, indeed, all about him, all of the time. But somehow the asshole embodies so much more beyond the mere façade of looking and acting stupid. This enigma of a person deserves a deeper dive of analysis into what makes up this phenomenal pest.

To go further, an asshole is the mindset of a person who triggers an attitude of false confidence, based on a lack of self-esteem, which attempts to predominate an environment of people as compensation for his inadequacy without purpose or cause, and as a result, is equally reckless with the damage he does to others. Much of what these people do to adversely affect us is intentional, and they do these things to assert themselves for themselves alone, at the cost of many others innocently affected. When an asshole sees that he does not fit-in, or that his ideas or behavior are not readily accepted or welcomed, or is not receiving the kind of personal attention he craves, this person will either lash out in a half-crazed expression of unbridled anger or store it in his repository of stale and envious feelings ready to burst in anyone's face without warning. And when they explode, it harms people in profound ways, like poison gas, suffocating any shred of liveliness in people.

Part of this problem also stems from the fact that the asshole doesn't know, or care to know, about how to harness and redirect, even dispel altogether, these expressions of anger and retribution. The inadequacy of the asshole looms so large that the idea of having him realize the damage he causes is well beyond his ability to ever comprehend it. Since childhood, the asshole has either been praised for achievements that did not deserve it, or deprived of praise for performances that did.

Put simply, as a child, this person has been praised for mediocre accomplishments that did not merit praise (or as much of it) as a compensating mechanism, or has been severely deprived of praises for reaching objectives that truly deserved acknowledgement. Praises and admonishments have worked at cross-purposes with each other for a long time. Either way, a frustration is born in him that grows and meanders its way through the years into adulthood, without really knowing the kind of person that he has become, who he is in the process, and what he does that harms us. And while it seems that he is numb to what he is becoming, this is not necessarily the case. Interestingly, the asshole understands he's a pest, he sees how he bothers people, and he knows that people don't like him. What he doesn't understand is that he's an asshole. In short, he doesn't comprehend the depth of his awkward inadequacy because he refuses to look inwardly to reflect on his behavior outwardly.

And so this person comes to us with an empty feeling of self, with a void in his chest too big to ever fill it, and attempts to get from others what he never got as a child no matter the cost. The asshole knows it, but covers it so that no one will ever know what he is. He is fearful of being exposed because he's come to know how others will respond to the truth of his persona. After all, it's what people come to know about themselves inside that makes them afraid; the asshole, in particular, is more afraid than most of us in the mainstream because he finally realizes what he's becoming at the surface, and, therefore, is ready to blast his bombast on anyone in his social circle or workplace who dares to expose him. Remember, these are equal opportunity haters, so without knowing how to redress his inane inadequacy, he recreates as a defense mechanism this outer personality into a mindset that projects, spews and sours onto people his brand of poison to whoever may try and stop him. His wicked awkwardness knows no conscience, remorse, or accountability for his actions, and they come to feel pretty good about it, too.

The asshole is a modern-day plague. He is a byproduct of affluence, created and molded by parents who have come to feel somehow entitled to something not yet pinpointed. As a consequence, he continues to be tolerated by his peers for sympathetic reasons or concerns over unexpected reprisals. The asshole can also come from meager beginnings as a "wanna be" but will "never be" kind of person, always ready to fight for his undeserved place in society. Cantankerous in nature and sanctimonious in attitude, the asshole is here to stay for a while. So, how do we pick him out from others? Well, you have to know what to look for.

Chapter-2

Characteristics

Everyone knows at least one asshole, and some people have the luck of knowing several assholes, but whether it's one or several, it's undeniable that their presence is everywhere. You find them in the workplace all the time, you see them in streets and in public places walking like arrogant lugs with empty looks and without purpose, and you may also come to have an asshole or two in the family as well! These endearing creatures of sweat 'n snotty noses are smudging up a lifestyle we've all worked so hard to get. Consequently, this is always a topic everybody knows about, but not everyone likes talking about it.

One of the most nagging questions among people at large is how to find these assholes and identify them for what they are. So, what do you look for? First, look for the <u>intellectual asshole</u>. You can find them by scanning for people who know what they don't know, but act as if they do. In short, you pick out certain personalities that seem to be smart enough to know about certain topics, until you realize they either have superficial "cocktail conversation," or they really don't know anything at all. Funny thing though, they're always aware of what they don't know, but need to pretend.

As a consequence of their flaw, they create a pretense of themselves and use it as catharsis for their fraudulent personas. It's like claiming to be the liberal who's really conservative because he's been busted for pot, and the conservative posturing as a liberal because his home has been bugged; this contradiction of character can only point to a person who has decided to repress who he really is in relation to what he knows, pretends to know, and does not know at all. This behavioral duality also speaks to the asshole that believes if you can't convince people of what others may suspect you don't know, confuse them. The obvious ruse can be very confusing for many of us because he has decided to intentionally mislead others into thinking differently about him to the point of rendering him inconspicuous. This also makes it difficult to know with whom you're dealing.

Second, look for a <u>fop</u>. These are the stylish assholes that have no style, no taste, and no perspective on anything. They misjudge social occasions by the manner in which they dress. They get the attention they need by standing out to others with color and print combinations that stifle the fluid ease of the eyeball. And the *pie`de resistance* is their touch of cologne, which wears as thick as napalm and whiffs like saran gas! They have no sense of how to wear a hint of a fragrance on the skin, with an aromatic pleasance that softly touches emotional memories cherished by many. Oh no! This guy, he splatters and drips on his clothes barrels of liquid stink, creating fumes that can even affect a neighbor's tonsils.

Another kind of foppish asshole quite common to us are those short and stubby pinpricks who stuff their fat faces with too many jelly doughnuts and coffee in the day, and then act as if they're on top of every situation. This asshole doesn't leave the house without first making sure he has these perfect little creases in his pants, that when combined with loud and colored undersized bow ties too small for his gummy neck, he gets looks from people like the faces you put on when dripping diarrhea. You will also find them to be either perfectly combed and groomed or dirty and smelly because their need to express extremes goes to the very heart of never commanding a perspective on anything relating to taste, class, art, conversations, sociality, and insights about themselves.

A particular problem the fop presents is that he uses his uncoordinated style of fashion and attire as a conniving mechanism to criticize others and make them feel bad about themselves. So if you dress like a rock star, an executive, a preppy professor, a conservative (whatever that may mean), or a relaxed garb for a beach islander, the fop will always find a way to ridicule you, your taste, and how you look in your clothes in relation to your weight. It's all designed to make you feel subordinate to him and well beneath his standards of appearances. The same applies to hairstyle, hair length, jewelry, shoes, in short: right down to your underwear!

And third, look for the <u>cretin</u>. This is the asshole that belly flops his oversized awkwardness onto people, like an immature little brother who creeps his way into adult interactions in social events for his own personal interest and attention. He will undertake outlandish acts just to get a laugh, such as imitate a stumbling paraplegic, run like a mentally disabled victim, or poke fun at the handicapped. This person has little notion of how uncomfortable he makes everyone feel in every social occasion that he touches. His behavior with people, either through distasteful and inappropriate remarks or acting out a latent adolescent condition, will quickly suffocate any remnants of civility left. It's like being locked in a room with someone you hate: you either want to stab him with your pencil twenty-four times or kick him once or twice just for good measure.

In parties or other social gatherings, he drinks when he knows he cannot hold his liquor, he dances when he doesn't know how to dance, he eats like a baboon, peeling and crushing his food as he slumps over his plate, mauling it over with a wide open mouth, up and down, round and round just like a concrete mixer. And of course, to go along with the trauma of his eating habit, pieces of food often drip or fall out of his mouth because of the enormous volume in it, expanding his cheeks with every chew to the size of golf balls on each side of his mouth.

To watch this guy eat is a freak show, not recommended for the faint of heart. Curiously, he pays no mind to the atrocity of his dinning etiquette, but he does watch others with surprising suspicion, as if to try to nab anyone who might want to steal his coveted cuisine. To further exacerbate his gluttonous moment, dessert time for the asshole is like ringing the dinner bell all over again. As if he hasn't had enough to eat (discretionary amounts are out the window with this guy), he continues his gorge among the several dishes offered all at the same time. Looking more like a man-o-war, he extends his tentacle-like long and grubby fingers to stuff his face with everything he sees.

But to watch this type of cretin dance is a real treat. No matter what the style of dance or genre of music might be, this asshole moves to the sounds he hears with uncoordinated motions of alarming proportions, creepy looks, stupid smiles, and pointless steps to the rhythm he impersonates. Honestly, it all looks more like a mating-call dance routine for rhinos in heat. His behavior is clearly beyond the realm of normalcy, and the disturbing part about all of this is that we're dealing with a real person here, not a person looking to imitate an asshole.

What does an asshole look like? Have you ever wondered? If not, prepare to be amazed. If you have, you may recall a certain style of appearance. He may appear to be oddly asymmetrical in body language. His posture when standing or walking is off-center; it's off-balance, because he doesn't know what to do with his arms and hands, so he swings them like a chimp and extends his gait as he slumps forward a bit in his attempt to strut. He wants to look cool and confident but comes across as a lowland creature looking about when making his way into a new world. And if he doesn't move his arms like a swing set, he wraps them up behind his head in an awkward effort to look relaxed and in control. Of course, this head-holding gesture only makes him look more nervous and insecure, but in his mind (and this is what many people have to understand), he needs to hyperbolize his persona to compensate for the inadequacies born and developed from early childhood.

To add more awkwardness to this contemptible enigma, the look of an asshole is also something to contemplate. These people, in their attempt to socialize, don't look - they stare. With sunken eyes, they watch many times in icy silence; they wait for an opportunity jump; and then with reckless disregard they splash into someone else's conversation with no particular purpose in mind. Interesting to note that his stare is not a malicious one, nor is it one of a walleyed pike either. It's a look that seems to go nowhere, disconnected, without focus, but one which is perceived to be odd and creepy.

His stare is also inscrutable because it often

reflects a perplexed mind that seems to have no direction, no place to hang one's hat, a ship that navigates without a port of call and finds no resolution in the everyday of his life. The asshole also has other stares that are bitter, angry, or sexually aroused too, but the one stare he gives off when sexually primed, let me tell you, is one that would rival Count Dracula when taking a drink. And, when the asshole starts to heave at the very thought of doing something with a nice girl he likes, the whites of his eyes in his excitement begin to flush red, giving his stare a sense of astonishment at the prospect.

And when the asshole dresses, it's unlike anyone else you've seen. Don't be mistaken with the way others dress in poor taste as well, no, no. A nerd has a distinct style, perhaps atrocious to many, but he's not an asshole when putting on his clothes. The flashy dresser, the pauper, the businessman, the pimp, the rocker, the bowling alley pullover of Wednesday night with the guys, the snappy pointed shoes, and finally, the discrete and low profile dresser, they all share a distinct style that go along with who they are as persons. Not so with the asshole. This guy has unusual particularities that annoy the view of normal people.

Starting with the top of his head, assholes

don't have any style in attending their hair. Nowadays, some guys ruffle their heads to give their hair a flustered or winded look to it. It looks cool when a person knows how to do it, and if one has the right kind of hair to do it with. But the asshole goes out with his hair looking as if he just got out of bed. His shirts, of questionable colors and print, are either too tight or too big, but the more pronounced part of his garb is how it all drapes on him: like dressing up a hog.

While most of us can wear t-shirts and look casually normal, the asshole looks like a large dog standing on his quarters with a t-shirt on. And the rest of him on down to his shoes is not much better. Often, the asshole wears a belt that fits two sizes too large, so what is left is about an 8" overlap of belt that just sags over the side. Usually wearing his belt tight, he sports a baggy pair of trousers that creases below the beltline too may times, giving him a look of an over-draped curtain. Since his pants drag all the way down to his shoes, it covers most of it. But the part of his shoes you do get to see peeks out of his overhanging pants like some furry critter looking to get out. Overall, his presence spells disaster for others, sooner or later. They can't help but be a nuisance because the asshole part of them is stronger than any other personal quality.

If you are careful enough to look for these three types of assholes, you have pretty much captured the vast majority of them. Knowing what to look for is almost half the battle, but if your scanners are alert, you'll flush them out quickly. And by the way, if you resemble any of these aforementioned characteristics, you'd best take a deep long look inside yourself: you may have something to think about.

Chapter-3

Where Are They?

The asshole is everywhere around us. He's the guy who repairs your car, the hotshot banker or arrogant lawyer that goes out of his way to make you feel insecure and dependent; the pig-headed executive who always has something to prove at the expense of others; the imposing in-laws, schlepping their fat asses into your living room with ideas of grandeur to redecorate your house; the oddball supervisor who presents himself publicly as innocuous, sensitive, caring, and collaborative, even inventive and funny, but is really a sour prick who isolates himself in his miserable hovel of an office because he has no social grace, and because he doesn't know what to do with himself when faced with real emotional challenges from people, and in the manure of his ways, he will always look for someone to carry the blame and burden for his maladjustments. We've all had supervisors like that in one form or another.

The asshole can also be your pesky neighbor who has mastered the ways of being a nuisance through either a yapping dog, loud and distasteful music, blocking your driveway now and again, encroaching in your yard with his big-ass truck, letting his dog crap on your lawn, or sounding off like a bullhorn when talking thirty decibels louder than normal. And after all these annoyances, he still quarrels with you occasionally in his pathetic effort to try to understand why you are being so difficult and intolerant.

This breed is also present in many school classrooms. This is the case of the overbearing teacher who has too much to prove to kids, a teacher who wants to be in vogue as their friend, who dresses and talks like they do, who interacts with kids - as a kid - outside the classroom, and a teacher who has decided to reject the notion that he will never be accepted as one of them. His inspiration to be "a cool teacher" with his students is badly jaded and fraught with misperceptions of what, in his mind, would've been a sure formula for success. And when it comes time to establish some sense of expectation and order in class, they all laugh. Why should he be surprised? This kind of asshole uses teaching as a power-position to verbally abuse students who don't agree with him, and in the process, imposes himself as a kind of bully in the classroom, and students quickly come to resent him.

Like the case of the teacher, you can also expect to find many other assholes with power positions in government jobs, private companies, large corporations, school administrations, and small businesses, all controlled and designed by them to make your life as a worker, partner, or employee miserable. Whether they come in the form of executives, board members, administrators, supervisors, department heads, techies, professional paper-pushers, or even the head of maintenance, they can all be problematic assholes. They carry private agendas, they all want to bully, and they are all either intellectual types, fops or cretin assholes who can't wait to taint your self-esteem, respect, and social circle.

Administrators of companies, hospitals or schools in particular, have a unique way of creating busy work for many while taking credit for reinventing the wheel, and they can care less about how others come to despise them for what they do. And by the way, don't misunderstand: the cretin, like the fop and pseudo brainiac, they're all there swelling up from the ground floor as well. Employees, like employers, owners, and everyone else who comprise the morass of bureaucracy, there is a mixed bag of assholes waiting for you at work. Remember that the asshole is self-centered by nature, so anything he does and continues to do is justified in the name of the lonely legend that he's created in his own mind.

One of the most dangerous moments is to watch how an asshole drives a vehicle on the road. Before you decide to observe this social phenomenon in progress, make sure you first keep a safe distance from him. Then observe carefully. He will cut you off in a second; he will weave the lanes of a highway as if he had the road to himself; he will pass you with a "fuck off" flicker of the royal finger if you're going too slowly; he will tailgate you, honk at you, harass you in creative ways all because he feels entitled and indifferent to you. Your safety and that of others on the road don't matter - only his own. He drives with a contorted look on his face like he's dripping brain matter on those cute little creases in his pants, as he pays no attention to the attitude of his driving, his aggressive turns, or his reckless disregard for road rules and laws. And if a police officer manages to pull him over for a citation, the asshole will do his very best to charm his way out of a ticket. Should his attempt fail, he'll go home and want to beat on his wife or girlfriend.

You also see assholes in movie theatres as they eat candy and popcorn while talking throughout the movie show; you find them as cashiers in food stores; trainers and muscle heads at the local gym; postal clerks in a post office giving you lessons on the virtues of postage in the age of emails; a car salesman, who can suck the air out of any room with his long-winded sales talk and cheap clothes, will make any car buyer scram for public transportation or wish for a bicycle instead.   But the best behavior ever experienced in your life has got to be from one's former spouse. Ah, ouch! Oh yeah, this guy can be a real winner! Almost always, this kind of asshole is a cretin who turns your life upside down in a constant torment. If he spies on you like the creep he is, he'll embarrass you frequently with what he saw in front of your friends; if he seems harmless and vulnerable at times, he's only recharging his batteries to launch an attack against you; if he remains quiet for a spell, he's getting ready to douse your kids with physical mistreatment; and if he sees you in a social gathering, he'll drink up a storm of regret only to spit at your face in his cretin rage.

Accountants, doctors of every stripe, psychologists, cops, salesmen, business executives, board members, architects and engineers, priests and rabbis, entrepreneurs, musicians, movie stars and directors, bureaucrats, clerks, athletes, military brass, politicians, farmers, crooks, in short: anyone of these can easily be an asshole. All he has to do is be himself because no matter how hard he tries to cover it, his true persona will always emerge. Remember, they're all around us. Just when you think you're having a normal day with normal people, there will be an asshole standing behind you, watching you with lurid looks and with an appetite to harm.

Chapter-4

What Do They Do? What Don't They Do?

What do they do? They annoy the hell out of people, but the asshole also knows his limits too. He will go as far as he can to annoy you, and then stop once you make clear to him your intention to no longer tolerate his annoyances. So, let's take a step back and think about these opening thoughts for a moment. The asshole, at the core, has always been insecure throughout his entire human development, and, as a consequence, has also suffered a profound lack of self-esteem. He sees the interactions with people as a parallax view of reality, a distorted or misleading amplification of human nature, in his efforts to try to understand them. He does not see a limit to his annoyance. What he does see, however, is a self-gratifying satisfaction to play, to capture attention, to elicit humor, and to annoy indefinitely. And if harm should result, he is indifferent about it.

At this point, if we decided to bring out his annoying qualities, he would not take it well because he would perceive it as an attack on his persona. If we don't point it out, he becomes relentless in his pursuit to annoy. Either way, an asshole becomes a problem. This is a guy who can care less about polite people, tramples on those who tolerate him, takes advantage of the weak and vulnerable, and shows no patience to those giving him advice.

So what don't they do? They don't challenge strength. If given enough confidence into your intimate circle of friends, the asshole will pursue you until there is enough reason in his mind not to any longer. What could be such a reason? Remember that the asshole is a scared mutt, so if confronted with a strong enough consequence to his behavior, such as the infliction of bodily harm or a serious enough outcome that stands to ruin his job or career, or even personal interests, he will make a U-turn. These people respond best to extreme measures, because they're mental clarity is not fluid, it's dense. And because of this density, their ability to discern is compromised and, therefore, judgment is clouded.

The asshole comes to find respect by way of deterrence, but not before first finding fear. Fear instills such an altered state of mind in the asshole that without committing to any rationale, he will choose distance before showdowns, if for no other reason than to protect his already dysfunctional matrix. Strength of character in normal people is perceived by the asshole as a juggernaut of complexities that he can't decode, and this frustration resonates deeply to the point of befuddlement and disillusion. Not knowing how to deal with strength, he lashes out to others of a more placid nature, and so his shit continues.

It's chilling to know that you wake up every morning to go to work or to be with family; the asshole, in contrast, wakes up to the same morning you share with him only to disrupt and annoy you everyday of your life! And why? Because there is an asshole in every corner of your day waiting for you, needing to soil up your day as he cleanses his with an insatiable appetite to be the asshole that never finds satisfaction in what he does. This is what you can look forward to when waking up every morning. I hope you have better things going on in your life to overshadow the darker parts of your day. I do wish this for you.

Chapter-5

How They Affect Us?

Assholes can affect us in many different ways and in many different scenarios. If you happen to work with one, he will always try to get ahead at the expense of anyone else because he is ambitious, but for all the wrong reasons. Since assholes do not normally team-up together for a single objective but rather, operate as a solitary breed, you will only be dealing with one asshole at a time for each scenario you face. They will throw you under the bus at the blink of an eye by concocting any story that will cast doubt on your veracity and integrity. And if successful, he will take control of circumstances and you will live under his tyranny at the workplace indefinitely.

At the office or in school, out in the field or in public plazas, the asshole will disrespect all protocols of professional courtesy and personal politeness. This is not a kind individual we're talking about here, so you really can't afford to overlook or underestimate him for any reason.

As a colleague or co-worker, he will conspire without motive; he will tell stories that will light you on fire; he will imitate the disabled just to get a laugh; and he will disrupt your work agenda to make you look incompetent with the work that you do. As a passive-aggressive being, he is a non-conformist, driven by personal ego, and never for a shared cause that is well founded for the needs of the many.

At home, if you're lucky enough to have one or two assholes in the family, they will go to the longest extents possible to make you uncomfortable. They do this because they know they are family members and as such, they come to feel totally free to disrupt your personal life because the family (in many or most cases) will accept them as they are. It's like saying, "We know he's a schmuck, but he's our schmuck," and this is all an asshole needs to hear from his family to make him feel entitled to annoy.

Former spouses have usually proven to be the most egregious assholes of all. When married, these people lack the spiritual seriousness upon which a marriage of two is founded: as one upon consummation. What they do instead is to create dependence for themselves while taking advantage of the other devoted spouse. The asshole is not equipped to see the beauty of a soul in love with another; he is unable to feel the rapture that goes along with the sharing of one's self to someone else, culminating in the unselfish joy of giving without expecting. The asshole doesn't see any of this; what he does look for, however, is a way to get what he wants, and he will stop at nothing to get it, either sooner or later. He will resort to cheating multiple times, hitting you, attacking your kids, neglecting his family, and even suing you in court for pennies on the dollar just to irritate you. And as he sinks and swims deeper into his world of Jack Daniels, everything he once had as uplifting and inspirational has now soured into a mish-mash world of shit. And he knows it but will never admit to it, because in his mind he is the victim to all of his troubled life. Even when he grows older and tries to change some of his ways, the "assholeness" in him will always prove stronger than he is, so he reverts back to his former nature and becomes a more grouchy and moody asshole who's become so bitter and brittle in his ways that there's no way to rescue him from himself anymore.

This is a miserable human being from the start of his life to the end of it. And along the way, he hurts people, both kids and adults, without care or conscience. The worst part about all this, is that his life, no matter how contemptible it may be, has become a product of his own doing: done by his own hand.

Chapter-6

Why Do They Survive?

Assholes survive because we allow them to. Yes, it's largely our fault for doing what we do that gives them longevity, and not doing enough of what we should do to stunt their growth. Their survival is based on our choice to either tolerate them or feel sorry for them. They, in turn, perceive this, and then move toward us with a semblance of appreciation, which is a false or misleading emotion on their part with the intent to deceive. Other assholes respond by affirming our tolerance and pity with an attitude of charming indispensability, such as, "You know you can't do without me" or "I'm practically irreplaceable to you and your family or organization." This "You need me" mindset will inevitably take ownership of you to the point of inescapability; it's a burden you'll carry for a long time, and it weighs heavier than a sack of elephant shit lumped over your back.

So how do we stunt their growth? Remember, the asshole respects strength. Unless you show him consistently a confident and staid condition of stern resolve, intolerance for the bullshit he spews, and showing the impatience necessary for him to realize a vague sense of limitation, his attitude will not grow very far. Assholes are like weeds growing in a manicured garden, and it isn't until you mow them down that their appearance will diminish. Important to note, however, that assholes, anymore than weeds in a garden, will never disappear completely. But as long as we can trim those weeds down to a bare-bone nub, we're ahead of the game.

And in case you're wondering why the asshole retreats from encountering a strong character? That's easy, he retreats because he doesn't know how to combat strength, how to respond, how to stay in the fight, how to suddenly preempt an adverse situation, how to keep a cool head, how to keep conscience out of an argument, how to maintain a laser focused stare when saying what you really mean, and even how to physically fight if it comes to that. For all these reasons, and possibly more, an asshole will retreat because he does not know how to win a confrontation; hence, his quick withdrawal from any showdown.

But many of us don't do enough of this because we begin to sympathize with a person who is so paralyzed in personality and so fractured in mental health that we coil up and extend a more tolerant disposition for him. And although this is quite humane, it's also equally risky. Don't forget that the asshole perceives all of this very differently from the way we do. While they are motivated to pursue weakness and exploit it at the right time, we are moved by the benevolence of helping another human being who cannot tell the difference between right and wrong behavior among people. And so, therein lies the trap: human weakness and foolish sentiment.

Assholes also survive because they are incredibly resilient. First, the asshole is not phased very easily when a particular situation is not going his way, and second, when they do get thumped, they jump right back as if nothing ever happened. As previously stated, assholes respect strength and quickly back down from anything confrontational, especially a sustained one. But anything less than a sustained confrontation does not leave a lasting effect on them because they don't process very well the purpose of the thumping in the first place. So they go on living, *ad naseum,* in their parallel universe of misfits, annoying us to no end, each day of our counted lives together. It doesn't look promising.

Chapter-7

Don't Get Confused

There are a great variety of people in the world, ranging from the street-smart individual and the intellectual snob to the more humble, the confident and the infinitely uncertain, the gay, straight, and the double hitter, the outgoing and the coy, the miser and the splendid, the fat and the skinny, the bitter and the laughable, the fanatic and the restrained, the angry and the poised, the patient and the rash, and so many more that it's difficult to keep up. But with all this variety of people, it doesn't suggest that they're assholes. We all share moments where even common folks act like assholes, where they throw a hissy-fit and take on the personality of an asshole, if only for a little while, and then they're back to being themselves again. These are the moments when friends say, "You're being an asshole!" in their moment of meltdown, but it doesn't mean they are one.

The asshole is still out there though, in respectable numbers and quite pervasive, so normal folks have to do a better job at discerning between the authentic breed and the "meltdown" impersonator. It's very easy to look and act like a real breed, and people can get confused at the outcome: understandably it's hard to tell the difference. Folks blow off steam all the time, but you know, it's ok to suffer a meltdown once in a while, now and again, because life is hard and full of stress, sometimes causing us to run off the rails a bit, but we clack back on and pick up where we last left off. So if we act like assholes from time to time as a release, well, ok then. But, we tend to remember who and what we are, and what we stand for, and that keeps us out of the abyss of the asshole.

By contrast, this contemptible breed of human does not know anything about himself, doesn't care to know, and couldn't give a rat's ass about what he stands for in the long and short of it. The satisfaction he draws from annoying other people is constantly short-lived because he can never be fully satisfied with his work of art, and so he drifts from one person to another to another, looking to replenish himself at a misdirected effort to please himself with what he does. Never a kind word, never a genuine gesture to anyone, this anomalous aberration of birth will stop at nothing, nothing, at inspiring others to follow the broken examples and fractured legacy they leave behind.

From the moment of their conception, they really are born as sons-of-bitches, and I'm not resorting to vulgarity here but rather, to the circumstances of their birth. What follows from this DNA matrix is a life full of maladjustments and dysfunctional behaviors that attack the mainstream of people like a swarm of maggots because they hate to see a confident and successful human being, and because they must predominate over such a person in order to be recognized and validated. Like shit-on-your-shoe, this detestable breed stays with you to smudge, to stink, and to alienate you from other normal people, if only for a moment.

So don't get confused from what they really are: definitely, a darker side of human nature. Normal folks act like assholes many times, and to an extent, they have good reason to act out. Whether it's an issue with the family or at work, tensions, antagonisms, and provocations do pull people apart periodically. But we also come to our senses sooner or later to re-glue what we previously tore apart. The asshole, well, he's the real deal because he has no past in his life, and he never looks back. Don't get confused between human nature and human perplexity, with the latter being immersed neck-deep in complexes and projected hatreds in the asshole.

Chapter-8

Their Usefulness

Can assholes be useful to us? Do they provide a utility that we can use to protect our way of living? That would depend on how much you choose to involve yourself with them. For folks who have more patience and insight into a variety of situations, certain people can use an asshole to influence a set of circumstances. By befriending them, they can remain loyal to that friendship for a while, and within the context of that brief collaboration the asshole can become an ally to spy, to disrupt, to annoy a competitor, to be the butt of a joke, or to support you by proving you right on a given point or situation. It all depends on how you use them, how you train them, how smooth you befriend them, and the kind of incentive you provide them for becoming your pet. Having an asshole on your side can be a formidable weapon as part of your arsenal to get ahead in life, but you have to know what you're doing to first win him over.

There are some sacrifices you can expect to make when winning over an asshole. First, you have to step into his world frequently. Vicariously, you must share together the same lens when looking at the world of people; you must pretend to understand and to agree with the same jaded convictions and criteria by which the asshole operates his sewage; and you must do it to the point of convincing him that you too are becoming an asshole, as a rite of passage, so there can be no mistrust or suspicion on his part. You must navigate these waters carefully, however, for if there is one slip up or miscalculation, the game is up. An asshole throughout this process of intimation will not betray you because these are lonely creatures at the core looking for affirmation. And when they begin to contemplate the prospect of a friendship together, they sparkle. Anymore than one can come to expect that "gator doesn't eat gator," the asshole will not take a bite out of you. So relax, remain confident and be calm.

Second, you must entertain the asshole, like the snake charmer who woos the cobra out of its basket, by keeping him confortable with a sense of humor that weaves him into a lull like a drug. Take a moment now and again to laugh at his schemes and stunts, to appreciate his sense of humor about life and people, and to make him feel that he makes a positive difference to people around him as he leaves his indelible mark, an autographic moment to be sure, in his monument of awkward arrogance. You must also time these strategies correctly though, so that your coalescence with him is perceived naturally and seamless. And, don't ever be afraid of losing your self-identity in the process of absorbing the asshole; remember that the asshole is a DNA born, defective and wrought-wrong, sociological byproduct that comes to you from a cesspool of shit and dregs, like zombies, looking for camaraderie and acceptance. Since your point of origin is nothing of the sort, you know how and when to pull your head out of the pit of the "ass-hole" anytime. Just be sure to clean up nicely before you greet someone normal again.

And third, you must replicate or commit to asshole behavior from time-to-time. By impersonating the asshole, you will have established a connection with him that will last for as long as you can manipulate him. When you start acting like an asshole, he will then laugh with you, commiserate and connive with you, all of his plans to undermine the rest of those outsiders who have shunned him in the past. He shares with you in this way because he feels so close to you now. This impersonation on your part also creates for yourself, an opportunity to take an inside look at what motivates and drives this person to weaponize his arsenal at hurting people as well.

What you see inside is what you can often control from the outside, and what you seek to control from the outside is not change (he is impervious to that), but rather a way to use his style of waging a nagging mosquito war on certain people that you may want thwarted. As a consequence, when people get exasperated with the asshole, they get unglued and begin to expose rash behavior and weakness, and that's the useful angle the asshole provides for you. Moving in on your competitor at this point and taking advantage of this situation may put you in a better place, thanks to an asshole! It is important to know that you need not sustain this effort at imitating the asshole frequently, but to do it once in a while does help consolidate the connection made with him and helps cultivate a trust that can remain intact.

The problem here, of course, is that not everyone is willing to take those steps, to dedicate time and patience in working one's efforts to achieving a good position on the chessboard. Many come to feel that all this is beneath them, that it's all a waste of time and resource, that it's too risky, and that you may never find a way out of your dive into this perpetual Black Hole. Perfectly understandable! This is not a natural act that people normally do, but for those whose penchant it is to delve into the extraordinary and unusual, this may be something to consider.

Chapter-9

How To Deal With Them

If you are not prepared or willing to make an asshole useful for yourself socially or psychologically, then you must be open to knowing how to deal with them when approached in social settings, work-related or familial in nature. It's never easy dealing with these personality caricatures because strategies that may work on one may backfire on another. It does help to know, however, that assholes respect strength, and they are also quickly discouraged to continue a pursuit of pestilence if they encounter a showdown with a stronger person. But once you spot them out, there are some steps you can take to ward them off like mosquito repellant.

First, you must put your best personal effort at ignoring him. I know it's hard, because the asshole does maximize his efforts to bother you. Since they are so good at it by nature, this is why you need to step-up your self-control in pretending he's not even there. There will also be moments when the approach of an asshole will come in the guise of a person in need, a friend looking for advice or consolation on something, and that's when he can also reel you in. You've now given him reason to depend on you, and like gum stuck to your heel, he will not let you go that easily. Remember the words of comedian Joe E. Lewis when he once said, "A friend in need is a pest!" And just like a pest, he will smell up your life with his infestation. It is therefore, paramount, that you find the strength to ignore him or stay as far away as possible so that there'll be no chance at all of meeting or talking with him. To do this effectively, you've got to have very good radar for assholes. Not everyone does.

Second, you can choose to do the opposite. Instead of ignoring him, relate to him on various points of conversation. But, keep conversations light and over the top, brief, and infrequent. There is a sage rationale in this piece of advice because the more asymmetrical you handle the asshole, the less predictable you become to him, hence, the more you keep him off balance and unsure. If, and when, you do decide to converse with him, find common ground quickly, and don't be disagreeable. Just dispense with the conversation at a bare-bone minimum and be done. As another alternative when relating to him, try finding humor in the asinine antics that he does by taking a moment to laugh at his jokes, no matter how distasteful and moronic they may be. Humor, in particular, is an interesting choice to use because it camouflages terrifically your defenses against him.

And third, smother him with kindness. This is the approach that has proven to be the most effective of all because it shows you're not intimidated by his incessant unruliness and rudeness, because you're not emotionally moved by the anger that drives him, and because you have chosen to not stoop down to his pathetic and reckless treatment of people. As stated in previous chapters, this is anchored as a behavioral issue, predominantly, which is why kindness, courtesy and politeness are the antidotes for the asshole. When using kindness, acknowledge his opinions and validate them, support his motives or causes, be impressed with his ideas, compliment his taste in clothes and art, encourage his feeling of entitlement, and create a façade of wonder about him as you feign your ruse into inscrutability. Killing him with kindness will make you totally enigmatic to him. Again, the value and benefit of being asymmetrical with kindness, relating humorously, or putting distance between you and him will create in his mind a question mark about you, a kind of deterrence that will eventually discourage, frustrate, and diffuse the asshole.

There is no perfect way of dealing with assholes in general, but there are methods and ploys one can certainly use to repel these people more often than not. This mosaic picture of deranged individuals can only be understood by examining closely their origins of misplaced feelings, frustrations, inadequateness, and depravity. These are the segments and patterns that grow into making an asshole, a very angry person at the core. He doesn't know how to exorcise or rid himself of this venom of insecurities and complexes that poison his life, so he lashes out with rudeness and aggressiveness to disrespect and belittle you, because he draws satisfaction at the cost of your esteem and self-respect.

Chapter-10

What Can We Learn?

When considering what the asshole has come to represent in all of its parts, we can learn, by contrast, to think more about ourselves, introspectively, about our humanity with others, and about how we want to be remembered in this world when our time here is done. The asshole is such an atrocious development of existence that this behavior should motivate us to learn other ways to become a better person for ourselves, our families, our co-workers and colleagues, and people at large. "Life is too short," as a good friend often reminds me, so we must expedite our learning to be better people with each other in the time we have left.

We all act out once in a while, only because it's part of who and what we are as human beings. But it also means that people don't want to be assholes or be labeled as one either. Sometimes, though, we do asshole things, and too often we do what an asshole does to the ones we love the most, which is astonishing. Without being assholes though, we are still rude to people in the everyday. We are vengeful, envious, intolerant, impatient, indifferent, cold, arrogant, malicious, confrontational, and even moody with each other without cause or reason because we are living as imperfect beings, and this is our flaw. The fact that we can recognize what we do and act out is not a sufficient enough lesson to learn; we have to do more than simple recognition if we are to really learn a taller lesson from assholes. In fact, we have to take the higher road.

Taking the higher road means that when they become narcissists, we respond with inclusiveness, thereby, bypassing all of the useless chatter aimed at justifying their exceptional attitude. When the asshole becomes impatient, we react with insight in redirecting their attention to something you want. When they become aggressive, confront them with an iron spine and they will seek shelter. And when they come to feel entitled, don't compete with their delusion by taking ownership of what they want at the moment: simply, invalidate the claim without any explanation.

Taking the higher road also means looking beyond the asshole to a bigger and longer-range understanding of our day. These people live for the here and now, the immediate and the instant, but when you take the long view on things, it now involves overlooking them without being distracted by their pesky behavior. Don't forget, assholes function on a different wavelength than us, which means they see themselves operating under a different moral structure than we do, and this is also why they come to feel impervious to our anguish with them and their inconsiderate entitlements to us. Since we don't want to be anything like them, we can learn to ratchet up our efforts to improve our behavior and outlook as well.

There is also, however, one more thing we can all learn the most from the asshole: how to get ahead. Remember that the asshole is eager to make an impression, he is highly motivated and driven to win your affection and acceptance, and in his journey to win you over, he becomes in the process quite passionate with the cause he pursues. This rapid momentum to seize their goal is further focused on the idea that they will stop at nothing to get what they want, be it a position at work, an increase in salary, a girlfriend or wife (can you imagine!), in short: an opportunity to control and consolidate power over people and situations favorable to them.

Assholes will do whatever it takes, without

restraint or compunction, to get to the top. And as despicable as this may sound because we are decent people of moral standards, it is nonetheless an admirable quality. While the moral turpitude of the asshole is an anathema for many of us, yet, it is precisely this quality of character in a world of tough choices and hard living that makes room for the asshole to get ahead. It's as if the world admires this limp and blubbery toad trying to make his way to the top of his career as he charms his adversaries and betrays his friends along the way. And the world laughs at this corky and awkward entity by saluting and rewarding his intemperate judgment and obnoxiousness to positions of power and responsibility. And when an asshole is finally empowered, there are problems for everyone.

So what can we learn from his drive and ambition? We can be reminded of a couple of truisms. First, personal ambition can never afford to take a day off. Just like the asshole, whose personality is geared and riveted, locked and loaded, with a relentless attitude to persevere and succeed all of the time, so must we forge ahead as well, and with the same appetite, too. Often, though, our days get sidetracked with other problems and distractions that pull us away from our focus to be more driven and determined in our ambitions but aside from this, we also lack occasionally the moral callousness that can turn us ice-cold in our pursuits, unlike the asshole who never falters. We are not always selfish and we don't carry anger issues either like the asshole, and we certainly don't act obnoxious in public, but should there be a chance to pick up a trait here and there from the asshole, perhaps we wouldn't have to see so many of them as managers, executives, and administrators of businesses, governments, and schools.

And second, because of his incessant socialization and contrived sense of charm on people, it can have a quick adverse effect. Every time the asshole preempts his bulging baggage of rhetoric so quickly on folks, it overwhelms them and doesn't give people a chance to process what's just happened. Perhaps the asshole has an inherited sense of timing, which we cannot replicate or imitate, but, it might also speak to value of such a method. How would we fare if we were to override certain points of a conversation with people while keeping a balance of civility intact? Could there be value in preemption?

The asshole, to be sure, does have some qualities that deserve scrutiny, which may warrant further consideration when foreboding his pathway to power. They are, for lack of a better thought, trailblazers, opening up a wider aperture of methods and style for our future. But do we really want to become like them? I don't think so!

Chapter-11

Signs Of The Times

This is not an apocalyptic time for the asshole, because he still survives. Whether by sympathy, luck, or destiny, this detestable stench of a person is found in every public and private place, ranging from banks, hospitals, and schools, to police stations, government offices, and professional firms; you can hardly start your day without running into one of them, often beginning with your next door neighbor! The current times, therefore, suggest to us that the only way to deal with this infestation is to assimilate it without getting too deeply drawn into asshole shit. How does one do this? You do it by learning how to deal with them. And if you don't want anything to do with them, go live on an island, grow old alone, and die.

Our society in its effort to be more democratic, accessible and decentralized has also made it more permissive for the asshole to make his way into our lives more frequently. It's an inescapable curse that we should share our existence with such a frog, and that people should entertain, in the name of "political correctness," a pest, whose only purpose in life is to be an irritant from morning to night. It's equally inconceivable to think that your most important collaboration at work might very well depend on an asshole; that business decisions may rely on an asshole; that important meetings are run by assholes; that critical surgeries may rest in the hands and mind of an asshole; that when driving home today, an asshole may dangerously cut you off or collide with you; and, if you make it home safely, an asshole member of the family is waiting for you just to make some needless irritating remarks and leave you with heartburn.

The signs of the times are also locked into the possibility that if a loved one requires immediate medical attention or surgical procedure, that surgeon in OR3 (operating room-3) may very well be an asshole. Let me say this again: you are placing the life of a loved one, or even yourself one day, into the hands of an asshole! Similarly, if you find yourself in a difficult legal situation, when friends and colleagues desert you, and there, in your darkest hour, when your only help and support (aside from family members if you're lucky) is a good lawyer to save you from the abyss of the underworld, that lawyer in that angelic hour of God's mercy to you, may very well be an asshole.

Our times today also reveal other interesting scenarios. When going to the dentist, for example, to repair or reconstruct a tooth, that sharp and spiraling rod that pierces your nerve in high-pitched screams, is the asshole autographing his name to the pain in your mouth. When you go to an expensive restaurant with your spouse for a nice quiet dinner, the noisemaker in the next booth, laughing loudly and recklessly to his heart's content without being considerate to others around him, is the asshole spoiling your dinner. When you wait for hours in a doctor's office without cause or good reason, what you finally get is a guy dressed in a tight and white medic coat who looks at your chart indifferently for ten minutes, never looks up, doesn't listen to what you're saying, doesn't care either, and when he gets tired of hearing your chatter he'll interrupt you abruptly, like crackling thunder, and walk away with remarkable aplomb. You've just had a visit from your doctor, who also happens to be an asshole. And when you are stopped by the police for going five miles over the speed limit and gives you a ticket just for having a clean record, he will not pass up the chance to also preach his green puke of macho shit to you about the importance of being a responsible authoritarian figure of the road for public safety's sake. The lucky part of your day was having to meet up with an asshole cop, not a police officer.

Similarly, the moment you arrive at a car dealer to buy a new car, the salesmen there will all go berserk at the first sight of you, as if they all short-circuited together, scrambling and blasting up against each other just to get your business. They all look like a bunch of bumper-cars on crack! You just know you're going to have a tough day getting a new car. And when you go to church or other holy place to have a moment with God, and you find yourself in the middle of a sermon by a clergyman who is more absorbed with himself than with God, singing and playing dissonance in celebration of his untalented fifteen minutes of noise, you'll know you're sharing divinity with an asshole.

If you take a moment to look around carefully, our times will always suggest that there are older civilizations in a state of decline and newer civilizations in a state of assent. But whenever anyone studies the causes and patterns of a declining civilization, one of the reasons for its deterioration, perhaps, might be attributed to the number of prominent roles that assholes have occupied and maligned in the wake of their tenure. And, once a civilization crumbles, the asshole, like a virus, moves on to the next burgeoning one. Although there have always been assholes in every civilization known to mankind, yet, the signs of our times today seem to point toward a record high level of assholes taking over powerful positions that stymie our way of life; alarmingly, this is a phenomena never before seen in other time periods. Mom, Dad, make sure that Susie or Jimmy don't marry assholes!

Chapter-12

Raising Awareness

You can no longer afford to go about your day with a general peace of mind. Unfortunately, you now have to be more tensely aware of the assholes in your day that will flush your morning, noon or night with their stench. So how do we raise awareness? Should we put up a big highway billboard with the face of a smiling cretin that reads "WANTED: DEAD ONLY!" Should we go on television and announce their whereabouts in commercials? Should we put up street signs in our towns that say "Caution, Drive Slowly, Assholes About."

What can we do with these people, really? How about putting up signs in stores and offices that say "No Assholes Allowed!" Should we fine an asshole for assholism? Should we use assholes as fair game during their high season of petulance (which is always) and sport them as we do quails? Should we do a rap song about the shit they do? Should we criminalize assholes? Can we deport them to the bottom of the sea? Can we send them off to war as frontline grunts and hope they get lost in the jungle? Maybe one of them can get in a fight with an orangutan and find him scared shitless up a tree? Can we send them to orbit on a NASA shuttle and lose them in space? How about creating a special traffic light for assholes, a light that twitches instead of flashes?

Maybe we should have a national holiday celebrating Asshole Day and as they parade in open cars, we can pelt them with eggs and tomatoes from rooftops to our heart's delight. Should we do a radio show jingle that harmonizes in poetic fashion the delightful pomp of their presence? How 'bout just tossing them in quicksand and offer a branch they can't reach? Should the United Nations create a separate country for them called the United Provinces of Assholes (UPA)? Can we let them go out and collect honey from beehives without protective gear? Can we possibly arrange for a raccoon to peek at a naked asshole taking a shower through a bathroom window? With any luck, he'll spot the raccoon, scream like a little girl, and slip on a bar of soap.

What if we have them collect golf balls on a driving range without the protective mesh on their little carts? How about if we watch them get chased by a gator when recovering golf balls from a pond on a golf course? Can we watch the beard of an asshole catch fire as he performs on a stage where the lights get too hot? Let's have the asshole feed the ducks and watch one of them take a shot at his pecker? How about going to a picnic and having him sit on a fire ant hill? Let's all sit on folding chairs and watch an asshole get chased by a cheetah as we sit there applauding the big cat? Let's go skydiving with an asshole and...? You think these ideas might work at raising awareness? Not sure, but it'll be fun doing and watching some. Ok, enough of this already. You get the point. Seriously, though, what should we really do about these people?

Short of going up to the rooftops and shouting "Watch Out For Assholes," there's really not much we can do to totally prevent their contamination. So be on the lookout and spread the word, that the asshole is here to stay, to marry into your family, to be a partner at work, to socialize and to break bread with you, and if ever you turn to him and say, "You look like I need a drink," he'll take you to a bar, get you drunk, and make you regret it for all time.

Chapter-13

The Danger

Life is hard enough as it is without having assholes in it, but once you begin to factor them in, you won't want to leave your house anymore. Simply put, the asshole is dangerous because he can harm you in profound ways that you would never come to expect. Think about the last time you were with an asshole doing whatever: How did he make you feel when with him, and how do you remember feeling after you left his presence?

The asshole has a remarkable talent to interject his stinger and leave you feeling dark and drained for the moment, but uplifted and liberated the next moment without him. His specialty is making you feel bad about yourself, and when his kind of fun is over, he bolts, because there is nothing left to feed off. This is a person who, in the process of making you feel like dirt, will disrespect your dignity and leave you to feel less than zero.

There are some people, however, who have a

stronger shield against the influence of an asshole, and so they interact with them under an almost immunized condition. But other people tend to take it more personally, thus, affecting their pride that comes with a history of lifetime achievements. Since assholes are not happy individuals by both nature and nurture, they will target those prototypes just to see anger poised up against an asshole's indifference and amoral disposition. Making you feel inferior to all the rest is how they come to be dangerous because what they leave behind after a storm of torment are people feeling fragile and vulnerable from the bullying experience.

Assholes can also make you feel weak and incompetent, and can even leave you to double-guess yourself over many situations. He impugns the authority of people whenever he can smell fear, insecurity, or intimidation. Like chumming the waters and ringing the dinner bell, the asshole will move in without compunction and rip you to pieces. Remember, this person has no conscience to distinguish right from wrong, appropriate or inappropriate, so what he does, he does for himself. He loves no one and he depends on no one; he protects his personal interests at all cost and relies on himself for everything. The asshole loves himself more than his own kids, his wife, and his mother. And it's quite possible that he loves himself more than money too. This compost-composite of a personality can have a devastating effect on people, almost to the level of a predator, but draped in a velvet dress. For all these reasons, and possibly more, the asshole is a dangerous person.

Chapter-14

Does Political Correctness Provide Protection?

This chapter examines the question of whether the asshole is protected under the aegis of political correctness. Being politically correct nowadays means having to use euphemisms for just about everything and everybody, because people have become so sensitive and so sanitized in referring to delicate or difficult situations, that honest and real conversations, or even jocular moments, have been sacrificed and replaced with a softer language aimed at protecting those who are easily injured and needlessly offended. It all sounds like crap: hypocrisy, at unprecedented levels! But for those who think that way, these are the folks who are prone to using the cover of political correctness as a cloak to protect the asshole from harsh language and other vicious attacks. As far as the asshole is concerned, he loves it because it protects him from what he really is. These are the people who protect assholes in this way, and they don't realize the harm they do by being politically correct with the wrong kind of person, instead of the right one.

There is a difference between being polite and being politically correct. Courtesy is for everyone to have with each other at all times, even when interactions become difficult. Being polite, as a measure of courtesy, is what ingratiates you with people in whatever endeavor you may share. Politeness is the confidence that comes from having social grace; it is, for all intents and purposes, the quintessential element that charms you in conversations. Political Correctness, on the other hand, is the excess amount of unwarranted sensitivity that comes from an effort to subterfuge in favor of an undeserved asshole. As a consequence, it misleads people into believing and defending a facade of protection for non other than a loathing asshole, while his real intent is to target you as the villain who preys on the helpless. Lately, there has been a turn toward courtesy, because people are becoming sick and tired of being politically correct all the time toward people that don't deserve it, like the asshole. This situation is turning the corner quickly against an unjustified correctness that has protected the unwanted and injurious behavior of an asshole for a long time now.

Perhaps many of you do not yet fully understand the conceptualization of political correctness in a broader context. Consider the following blog recently written by this author on this new form of PC expression and hopefully you'll be in a position to better comprehend the tragic misnomer behind political correctness: insidious incorrectness:

On Being Politically Correct

A Rant

The First Amendment has lately become a stronger way of life for us, especially in our time of "identity politics," where free speech is on trial and its future, uncertain. We rely on it for guidance, we look on it faithfully as an answer to our diversity somehow, and so we as a people continue to live our lives with presumptions of freedom, acting as a safety net toward our denial of the truth.

As a free people, Americans have a long history and heritage, even a habit, of making unfettered choices for ourselves and our families, of freely expressing opinions and convictions to friends and colleagues alike, debate contentious issues of our choosing without fear of reprisal, even to fight for the right of the other guy to speak on opinions you disagree on. At least, this   is what we have bragged out for centuries; this is what makes us proud; this   is also part of what we have imposed on others throughout the world as a means of extending to uncivilized peoples, the blessings of our democracy and speech. This is our brand – the freedom badge of arrogance – from which it is also well earned over the many wars fought, but less deserved when considering the manner in which we have decided to exclude unequally, the right of inclusivity among ethnics and races right here at home. And while it is a good idea to guard the inclusiveness of the many, still, this right of ours to speak freely continues to ring hollow when compared to the blinding brilliance of real free speech.

To speak our mind in a free society is a gift that is given to us each day. Lately, however, there is good reason to feel somber about the chances at achieving real individuality. We are somber at the thought of preferring to remain silent in conversations that predominate with a particular neoliberal perspective for the sake of avoiding nasty fights, instead of exchanging differing points of view without the insults. Being mutually tolerant of each other really is being politically correct if it is to be a truly free society, but when people use our rights as a bedrock to advance a totalitarian point of view at the cost of others who dare challenge it, it is no longer a First Amendment nation: it's something else: we are becoming something else.

We are also frustrated at the thought of knowing that over-sensitivity on issues is tethering many of us from freely expressing how we think. We're tired and angry at the possibility that there is waiting out there, even lurking, a pseudo "politically correct" police of crypto fascists monitoring all of us, ready and anxious to pounce on anyone who dares to express a counter, or otherwise, different point of view on issues against the imposing, intolerant, and pervasive neoliberal perspective. Conservative or moderate voices are rarely welcomed in their abysmal tyranny of public opinion.

These are the maggots that patrol the airwaves of television and social media, always lurking, always anxious, like hungry wolves looking for a meal, to see whom they can snag into their snare of malice. These people are forever busy in finding ways to dislodge and reconfigure the matrix of our First Amendment history, and they will not rest until the damage done is irreparable and irreversible. These pseudo "PC" groups of neoliberals won't hesitate to stone you at every turn, and with dark hearts in their speech will that intolerant police drown and devour the last of a remaining memory of a free republic.

Today, giving a compliment on anything can no longer be safe either; we all have to look a little bit over our shoulders to see who's around, or how your compliment is being received, perceived, measured and weighed by the other person. Thoughts like "What did he mean by that," or "Is he trying to insinuate something?" are thoughts that create paranoia if left undetected long enough. Folks, human nature isn't that complicated, for one does not need to over-analyze a simple compliment. This may sound extreme for some, but the extreme has become the norm, and it's also becoming difficult to even converse with people. A moment will come, I fear, when conversation in the conventional sense will diminish for two reasons: first, the risk of being labeled, judged, or falsely accused of something is too great, and second, disillusionment will get people to think that it's just too much effort to simply chitchat with anyone, anymore.

In the workplace, forget about criticizing a colleague or co-worker for something done wrong or incorrect: much too risky! You have to use veiled language to point something out and then, hope the other person understands and doesn't take it personally. In schools, as in corporations, instruction and management are compromised and truncated, learning and discipline are biased and diluted in the classroom, the work ethic of employees in the workplace has been replaced with complacency, and managers as well as administrators have long abandoned the interest of the client for job security.

In universities, free debate, conviction and creativity are all under arrest. The university classroom in particular, once thought of as a laboratory of democracy and free speech, has become totalitarian centers of controlled thinking by professors and students alike. Even in workplace gatherings, social talk has been confined and reduced to mere nubs of unimportant gab because people are afraid to speak up about what is wrong.

And at home, be careful with what you say to a son or daughter, stepchildren, grandkids, cousins, even Uncle Buck: it might get you in trouble, too. The workplace, like the home in certain ways, have always been considered "safe zones" for commentary, gossip and other minutia but today, the home in particular has also become a place where political correctness, expressed by misfits and loners of high caliber, have come to find catharsis in clamoring for the public execution of what may still remain as the final vestiges of that iconic prayer of American Exceptionalism: free speech!

From the blog, the question that should preoccupy us is, how dangerous is political correctness, and whom will it protect the most? Free speech is in danger, and political correctness is the filter that suffocates our right to speak out. As complicated as our society has become, and with assholes running all over the place like horny jackrabbits on the fritz, we now have to contend with this PC development. It has become impossible to even breathe without having someone tell you to breathe in another direction, because it's PC proper to recognize the airspace of someone else, perhaps that of an asshole!

So with political correctness running amuck, who do you really think is going to take full advantage? My bet is on that racehorse in the fifth called "asshole." For everything that PC culture has to offer, it is a sanctuary for the asshole, and they will stop at nothing to protect the PC environment of sponsors as long as it still remains in their interest to do so.

Chapter-15

Elohssa Therapy?

Can we do something to protect our sanity against the sinews of an asshole culture gone mad? The answer is yes. We can take up Yoga, meditate on assholes, and breathe our anxieties in and out for a predetermined period of time (be careful in the direction you breathe) under dim candlelight and funky music. You can also have little dinging bells to alert you when its time to return to the assholes. Oh, and be sure that when folding your body into a pretzel, you don't slip a disc, and don't get lice on your hair either.

We can work out in the gym. Exercise has often helped exorcise tension, so people do it all the time. You can walk or jog on a treadmill until strings of sweat dangle down to your big toe and your skin face dips a quarter inch, leaving you with sunken eyes like that of a terrorist or drug addict. Your testicles may also suffer a bit of a dip because of the constant rub on them, but it's of no consequence: after all, we're concentrating on our sanity, not our gonads.

We can also lift weights! Ah, yes, this is where people have the most fun. In order to lift weights effectively, you must carry in your mind a motivator to lift where no man has lifted before. What's the best motivator? Think of an asshole! And if you let that memory simmer and stew long enough, then you're ready to lift. You start by taking deep passionate breaths, as if you're ready to have sex with an ugly woman, and then scream! And with eyes bulging, veins popping, arteries exploding (forget about your testicles now) and your body twitching like a chicken without a head, you lift the asshole up and down, up and down, up and down again until you throw the asshole to the floor and finish him off with a final yell and a spit to him. After all that, we feel pretty good about it.

If lifting weights isn't your thing, we can play a sport. Take your pick from among so many of them out there. But also remember that you may be playing against an asshole. You'd be surprised how many of them are out there who also want to compete. Now you not only have to deal with them mentally and socially, but physically too. No matter what game you play, the asshole will be there pulling on your shirt, tucking on your pants, pulling your socks down from mid-calf to your ankles, giving you head-butts now and again, tripping you, elbowing you, taunting you, talking smack, kicking and even hitting you with his stick, depending on the sport. He will foul his way through every game for as long as he can get away with it. After all that, don't know if you want to sport with them anymore.

If you are not into sports that much, here are a list of other hobbies or distractions you may consider doing as therapy against assholes. You can play Ping-Pong, although the pong in missing the ball will frustrate you more than the ping in scoring. Just don't hit anyone in the eyeball. You can pace up and down at your leisure and to your heart's content, but be aware that others are watching you turn weird; you can pray in the name of the asshole, his son, and to his posterity to be spared of his annoyances; you can pick up dancing and learn to do the Hucklebuck; try holding hands with other people in a group and sing Kumbaya together; try biting your nails down to the bone; ride your bicycle in city traffic and join the road-rage gang to see who can flick their middle finger the highest; try doing the Hokie-Pokie and move it all around, "that's what it's all about"; talk to yourself – many people do, and they have one hell of a conversation with who the hell knows; you can create little asshole manikins and torch'em on the barb-b-q; you can pop out your blackheads to release tension; pick up singing even though you're tone deaf, or learn to play the oboe (don't know why you would); try doing the mambo, get yourself religion and shave your head or play bongos in a church and hit a tambourine twenty thousand times a day praising God; you can also become a cloistered monk forever. And after dealing with assholes all day long, there might just be a justification to drink, because for those who don't, that's as good as you're going to feel for the rest of the day. You can engage in a series of entertainments for therapeutic value, some more eccentric and dangerous than others, granted, but there's always something you can do. But the question really becomes one of realistic expectation: will any of these activities work? Probably not. So, what will?

The best therapy against assholes is the gravitas in you. It comes from having the confidence of knowing whom you are inside and what you stand for in your life. It has often been considered that if you want to be happy and successful, you have to practice success everyday; this also means that you learn the most about yourself by the failures you practice everyday as well. Your failures will give you success in becoming an enlightened human being, and from your failures you will also be able to forge the capacity of reflecting inward. To have the ability to look at yourself in difficult moments with other people is to never lose yourself. A man of faith, spirituality, conviction, humility, and courage will always know what he is in all moments that temper his character, and this is more than enough to fend off any and all assholes that dare challenge the titan in the rest of us. And as far as those remaining assholes in the world, the titan in us must find a way to validate them, because at the end of the day they are human beings that belong to God, and all life must be respected.

Leadership comes with great responsibility, and so we must carry the onus of treating our fellow human beings, including assholes, with the dignity that every person deserves from all walks of life. Wisdom is the insight that comes from experience, and if our experiences have taught us anything worthwhile, then the insight that makes us wise to the ways of the world must also keep us on a steady course throughout the years, with enough balance and perspective to continue to reach out to those who still remain unable to understand the community of people: the asshole.

I would like to leave you with one final thought as this story comes to an end. Think about this when you go to bed tonight and then dream of living a long life: "May you live for a hundred and fifty years, and that the last voice you hear in your mind is mine, ever so quietly whispering to you, 'watch out for assholes'!" Good Night!

About the Author

Once, my father asked me what I wanted to be when I grew up. Being very young and quite impressionable about teachers, I didn't give him the answer he was hoping for: a lawyer. But as the years passed, high school came and went just as quickly and before I knew it, I was in college. Not prepared, and even less motivated to take academic responsibility seriously, my brother approached me like a lightning rod and insisted that I start studying now, and that I <u>must</u> become a teacher. This attack came to me, of course, the minute my first semester college grades reached our mailbox: the grades were not encouraging at all.

What struck me the most about my brother's tirade was his incessant drumming into my head, the idea of becoming a teacher. That idea kept me curious for a while, even made me reflect back to when I was a boy, remembering this great admiration I had for teachers. Impressed wasn't enough of a word when it came to them; I was simply dumbfounded by the manner in which teachers controlled an entire class of kids like me, can grade so many papers and still maintain a sense of fairness, how a teacher came to be so knowledgeable about so many things, and such good speakers they had to be in communicating information to their students. Teachers were, in a word, role models for me as an elementary child.

I came to learn later through social gatherings and some family history, that my mother was a teacher for many years, my first cousin was a teacher, my paternal uncle was a university professor, my paternal grandfather was also a university professor, and my great, great, uncle (uncle to my paternal grandmother) was also a university professor. So what I never thought about before, I now began to consider seriously, especially with this kind of lineage. As a young man in my early twenties, the idea of becoming a teacher began to sound like a cool thing to do, a neat "gig" for the moment, vacation time was attractive, and I would be finishing the day early. But I still wasn't totally sold on the idea yet; I had uncertainties that continued to keep me at bay. Mainly, the preoccupation of whether I had the right capacity, temperament, and condition of character to do all those things I so much admired in my elementary school teachers. I had plenty of doubts.

It wasn't until finishing my undergraduate degree, and with no other job prospects in the horizon, that I decided to apply to my first school in August of 1977 for a grand yearly salary of $5,500. Needless to say, the salary was a disappointment, but there was another side to this prospect that had me intrigued about the challenge that waited. Being a little older now, I began to take a more sobering look at the prospect of actually becoming a teacher, of becoming this role model I had long admired, and all of the sudden it all seemed possible to me, so I started to take more of a personal interest. I became a teacher. The devotion to impress upon younger students the righteousness, morality, and sanctity of knowledge was exciting and overwhelming for me. I can still remember classes where discussions from class projects became inspirational moments of learning for everyone there, and to be at the center of it all like a symphony conductor, is a God-given memory that will never tarnish. Since the fall of 1977, I have been a teacher for almost 42 consecutive years now, and a small business owner of a national tutoring franchise for the past 3 years.

I've also had, riding along side my teaching career, this love for music that I got from my mother, who was a guitar instructor and occasional performer for over 60 years. In my early thirties, I use to sing American standards with a simple quartet in private parties and small bistros, performed karaoke's in very few clubs around town, and did some recordings. The musical stint, however, didn't last very long because it wasn't proving to be a lucrative experience for the few years I did it. Oh, but I really did love to sing old Frank Sinatra crooner melodies, Julie London tunes, Peggy Lee songs, and so many others that it made me sing as a minimalist performer. A soft melody line with an occasional tinkling piano and an upright bass that gave a tenor sax a reason to speak low, were all moments of transcending to another place. It was simple and beautiful. And, oh, how the audience loved it! Great times for cherished memories, but it was time to move on. Even now, you can still catch me singing a tune alone in the car now and again.

At the time, I thought it'd be best to go back to school to finish a master's degree and a Ph.D. At the moment, however, I still have oral exams and dissertation work pending. Since then, I've been working in the classroom, both at the high school and university levels in various schools. Also in 1999, I had the distinct honor of being chosen as the recipient of the prestigious Deaver Foundation Award for Teacher of the Year. It was a national recognition that awarded me $1,000 in cash for remarkable work in the classroom. It was a humbling and surreal moment, for sure. And although I've had an incredible run as a teacher, there have also been moments of formidable challenges. For every three steps I took forward, I had to occasionally take one or two steps back. Why?

Throughout my career, I have been involved in many interesting situations with assholes of different stripes, and so I find myself inspired to share these experiences with others in order to raise a new level of awareness regarding the threat that assholes present, and the humor that it all comes to represent for all of us at the end of the day. When starting out as a young teacher, there were assholes telling me I couldn't teach well; whenever I went to another school as a new teacher, there were new assholes showing me the wrong way of doing school work and conniving against my best efforts to improve as a teacher; when I started singing and recording, there in the crowd were asshole hecklers discouraging the mood of a song; when returning to the university to complete my academic studies, asshole professors would impose their opinions and manipulate discussions to make me and others feel stupid and incompetent; when I was department head of a private school, I had a major asshole of the cretin type, that was always conspiring against me and my efforts to lead the department for thirteen years; and no matter what school I ever worked at, there were assholes everywhere. Always thinking they knew it better than anyone else, they never failed to come along with their disdain and contempt for people and smother their arrogance on everyone with personal recklessness and a condescending disregard for humanity.

Through it all, I've come to see what assholes can do to people. I've seen the hurt and the pain, the anger and the frustration that assholes can provoke and cause onto others without reason. I've also come to see the anxiety and violence that cretin assholes can cause as in-laws in the family, particularly from son-in-laws, that can rip apart the innocence of a child at the cost of their insatiable and lewd satisfaction. It is because of these contemptible demons that I write this book, in the hope that we all make a taller effort at growing up a little more in order to oversee the asshole, but not overlook the beauty of life, God, and the love within us.

Made in United States
Orlando, FL
13 November 2024

53865387R00062